You Know You're a
Rugby Fanatic
When...

Steven Gauge

summersdale

YOU KNOW YOU'RE A RUGBY FANATIC WHEN...

Text by Steven Gauge

Illustrations by Roger Penwill

Summersdale Publishers Ltd
46 West Street
Chichester
West Sussex
PO19 1RP
UK

www.summersdale.com

Printed and bound in China

ISBN: 978-1-84953-045-3

Substantial discounts on bulk quantities of Summersdale books are available to corporations, professional associations and other organisations. For details contact Summersdale Publishers by telephone: +44 (0) 1243771107, fax: +44 (0) 1243 786300 or email: nicky@summersdale.com.

You Know You're a

Rugby Fanatic

When...

Your fragrance of choice is Deep Heat.

Your Facebook profile picture is a close-up of your latest injury.

You consider an uncontested scrum to be like a day without sunshine.

You put international rugby fixtures in
your diary before your
family's birthdays.

You find yourself recruiting players at work, social events and even approaching random rugby-looking types on the train.

The IT department at work wonders why your Internet history includes a YouTube video entitled 'Massive Tackle'.

11

You find it hard to order drinks at a bar in anything smaller than a six-pint jug.

Your wife sells the contents of your kit
bag at the local garden centre
as topsoil.

You teach your children to hate Australians from a very young age, in order to save them time later.

15

You know all the words to 'Swing Low
Sweet Chariot' and 'God Save
the Queen'.

You don't feel properly dressed unless you have three metres of tape strapped round your head.

Your collar size has come of age.

You can carry six pints in between two
rows of fifty seats without spilling
a drop.

You aren't in the least bit embarrassed when your coach asks you to show him your tackle, and make it hard.

You can't pass the salt without
throwing your outstretched body
halfway across the table.

You know alternative, very childish sets of lyrics for 'La Marseillaise', 'Flower of Scotland' and 'Land of my Fathers'.

Your ears count as one of your
five a day.

You know the name of every muscle in your body – despite having failed GCSE biology – because you have pulled them all at some point.

Your joints are mostly held together
with neoprene.

You are banned from school sports days for tackling the other competitors during the fathers' race.

Your GP refuses you any further
treatment until you show her a letter
of resignation or expulsion from
your rugby club.

You spend an entire afternoon learning how to make a PowerPoint animation work just so that you can demonstrate the new line-out moves to the rest of your team.

Your boots are mostly held together by dried mud and gaffer tape.

You miss the deadline for filing your tax return because you have a match report to write.

You find yourself enjoying the relative comfort of the London Underground in the rush hour after an afternoon on the terrace affectionately known as 'The Cowshed'.

You start trying to sidestep random strangers as they are walking towards you in the street.

You are able to ask other men if you can borrow their pot of Vaseline without any sense of embarrassment.

Your physiotherapist books a 5-star holiday in the Bahamas.

Your osteopath starts driving a Bentley.

Your dentist has a nervous breakdown.

Your wife appoints an interim husband
during the months from September
to March.

You know your way to all the rugby clubs within a 25-mile radius but aren't entirely sure where your parents live these days.

You only ever remove your mouth guard in order to abuse the referee.

You believe that most medical conditions can be cured by the application of a wet sponge from a bucket of cold water – for everything else there's alcohol.

Your friends keep your photograph on the mantelpiece to keep the children from going too close to the fire.

You think that a late tackle is defined only as punching someone in the bar after the game.

You find small pieces of ear – and other body parts – stuck between your teeth.

You realise that the only reason 'What goes on tour, stays on tour' is that everyone was too drunk to remember whether there was a tour at all.

You need to have at least three simultaneous injuries before you tell your captain you can't play.

You add PlayStation karaoke to
your training and fitness regime in
preparation for the club annual dinner.

You have rugby Alzheimer's – you forget everything but the grudges.

Your wife complains that you know more moves for the line-out than the bedroom.

You arrange a fixture against the local
netball team, and still lose – but the
post-match bath is more fun
than usual.

You look forward to turning 35 so you can finally play for the veterans' team legally.

You don't need a costume to go to Halloween parties – years of heavy tackles have seen to that.

You have to break for orange segments halfway through any physical activity – running for the bus, climbing the stairs, having sex.

You own more replica shirts than work ones.

You are happy when it rains during the week because that means a softer landing when you are tackled at the weekend.

You think that the only thing spoiling the national game is the length of the British summer.

You and your fellow supporters can have a beer or two at the ground without starting a riot.

You finally learn to love the rules that mean your team can finish top of the league but lose the title in the play-offs.

You've been to more gala dinners with John Inverdale than with your wife.

You feel lonely in a bath on your own.

For some reason when you wake up on a Sunday morning during the rugby season, your car is never outside your home and only your local taxi driver knows why.

You postpone your retirement at the end of every season by buying a new pair of boots in the sales.

For you, a conversion is the act of discovering a distant Welsh great-great-grandmother once you have failed to make it into a southern hemisphere international team.

You may have had three wives, eight different jobs and ten homes, but you'll only ever have one rugby club.

You take a Masters degree in Euclidean logic in order to understand the new play-off system.

You are under the misapprehension that a giant foam jester's hat in your team's colours is an acceptable form of headwear.

Your autographed programme
collection includes William Webb Ellis'
end-of-term report.

Your idea of a romantic Valentine's weekend trip is to either London, Rome, Paris, Edinburgh, Cardiff or Dublin – depending on how the 6 Nations games are scheduled this year.

You are under the mistaken impression
that your job in the terraces is as the
referee's assistant.

You find yourself watching a group of South Africans playing in Reading but can't work out why they call themselves London Irish.

You persuade your council to name the local public convenience, built with a traditional brick finish, as the Jonah Lomu Loos.

You find yourself agreeing with Brian Moore more than once in a game.

Whilst watching rugby at Bath, you can't decide whether the ground's nickname 'The Rec' is short for recreation ground or recreational drugs.

You find yourself sitting in the middle
of a group of vampires, but relax
when you realise you are watching
the Harlequins.

You've been sent off so often that every time you hear a guard blow his whistle at the train station you get up, go home and get in the shower.

You take out an injunction to stop your wife coming within five metres of the remote control during the Rugby World Cup finals.

Have you enjoyed this book?
If so, why not write a review
on your favourite website?

Thanks very much for buying
this Summersdale book.

www.summersdale.com